The American Poetry Review/Honickman

First Book Prize

The Honickman Foundation is dedicated to the support of projects that promote spiritual growth and creativity, education and social change. At the heart of the mission of the Honickman Foundation is the belief that creativity enriches contemporary society because the arts are powerful tools for enlightenment, equity and empowerment, and must be encouraged to effect social change as well as personal growth. A current focus is on the particular power of photography and poetry to reflect and interpret reality, and, hence, to illuminate all that is true.

The annual American Poetry Review/Honickman First Book Prize offers publication of a book of poems, a $3,000 award, and distribution by Copper Canyon Press through Consortium. Each year a distinguished poet is chosen to judge the prize and write an introduction to the winning book. The purpose of the prize is to encourage excellence in poetry, and to provide a wide readership for a deserving first book of poems. *In the Surgical Theatre* is the second book in the series.

T0160627

IN THE SURGICAL THEATRE

IN THE
SURGICAL THEATRE

POEMS BY

DANA LEVIN

WINNER OF THE APR/HONICKMAN

FIRST BOOK PRIZE

THE AMERICAN POETRY REVIEW

PHILADELPHIA

Direct all inquiries to
The APR/Honickman First Book Prize
The American Poetry Review
1721 Walnut Street
Philadelphia, PA 19103

Distribution by Copper Canyon Press/Consortium

Library of Congress Catalogue Card Number: 99-72580

ISBN 0-9663395-2-5 (cloth, alk. paper)
ISBN 0-9663395-3-3 (pbk., alk. paper)

First Edition

Designed by Cynthia Krupat

ACKNOWLEDGMENTS

Thanks to the editors of the following magazines, where some of the
poems in this book first appeared (at times in different forms)
or will be appearing: *Ploughshares:* "Wind," "The Baby on the Table";
Boston Review: "Lenin's Bath"; *Prairie Schooner:* "Marvelous Father,"
"Body of Magnesia," "In the Surgical Theatre"; *New Letters:*
"Movie," "Bathhouse 1980"; *Countermeasures:* "Personal History,"
"Door," "First Cradle," "The Nurse," "Chill Core,"
"The Problem of Light"; *Sojourner:* "Sleep"; *Global City Review:*
"Field"; *Pequod:* "Fever"; *Third Coast:* "Banishing the Angels";
The American Poetry Review: "The Work."
"Door" appears in *Pushcart Prize XXII.*
The Quest of the Holy Grail is translated by P. M. Matarasso.

Endless gratitude to the National Endowment for the Arts for a 1999
Literary Fellowship; and to Richard Tayson, Malena Morling,
Gretchen Mattox, Jeanie Tietjen, Bex Wilkinson, the Saturday Morning
crowd at Muddy Waters, the editors at *APR,* Lynne Honickman,
the Vermont Studio Center, the Ucross Foundation, my family, and
Louise Glück, who gave time, insight and care to the final editing
of this book—and to Barry Sanders, Charles Simic, Greg Glazner,
and Jon Davis—for opening doors.

CONTENTS

BODY

LENIN'S BATH · 3

EYELESS BABY · 5

BATHHOUSE, 1980 · 7

BODY OF MAGNESIA · 9

PAUL, ROOSEVELT ISLAND · 10

THE NURSE · 12

THE BABY ON THE TABLE · 13

IN THE SURGICAL THEATRE · 16

Personal History · 21

HOME

FIELD · 31

SILO · 32

WIND · 34

SLEEP · 36

CHILL CORE · 38

HIS DEFENSE · 40

FEVER · 42

WING · 44

MAGPIE · 46

HIVE · 47

DOOR · 49

The Beautiful Names · 51

WORLD

SMOKE · 59

POWER · 60

MARVELOUS FATHER · 61

FIRST CRADLE · 62

THE PROBLEM OF LIGHT · 68

MOVIE · 70

BANISHING THE ANGELS · 73

WITNESS · 74

The Work · 77

INTRODUCTION

BY   LOUISE   GLÜCK

Frank Bidart has remarked of the poet David Matias that he wrote as one in the grip of a story. In Matias' case, the story was AIDS, its power simultaneously destructive and generative.

The remark can be adapted to describe Dana Levin's first collection. For *story* substitute *image*: at the book's center (and reaching into all the surrounding material) is the surgical theatre, an image, like Plath's bees, metaphorically fertile, its manifold resonances revealed through Levin's extraordinary and demanding intelligence. The danger of such powerful figures is the danger of lesser imagination, imagination content with the first circle of revelation. What in such a smaller talent might have proved repetitious, banal, self glorifying, is, here, the heart of an astonishing book.

The richness of its center derives from ambiguity: the raised scalpel— healing that looks like assault. A healing, an assault, aimed, often, at a baby, so that the hovering knives become at once an image of salvation and the first impression of a lethal world. The recurring figure has the feel, or, more accurately, the force of biography, of lived experience. But it is biography wholly transmuted into metaphor, which is to say Levin's experience (whatever it is, whether she is patient or surgeon) is life not simply lived through but thought through: the authority of the real combined with the larger evocativeness of imagination.

> Do you know if you want it? Is that jumble of spit and bone
> so worth it
>   that you would go down again and be
> a body
>   raging with loss, each beat of the heart
>
> like the strike of a hammer,
>   spiking the nails in, to feel, to *feel*—
> I learned this from you, Father, all my life

I've felt your resign to the hurt
of living,
         so I came up here, to the scaffolding above
the surgical theatre

         to watch you decide.
Can you go on with this mortal vision?

The book begins, though, in disturbing tranquility:

         The assistants lift him gently,
gently. For a moment, the one lifting under his arms
         is in the attitude of an artistic
sorrow—It is
         the Deposition, the taking down of the god.

In the stillness of death, there is activity. Less violent than the scalpels of heal-
ing, but more assured as to outcome:

         When they've gone, Debov sits watching. He imagines
the sheath of bacteria he knows is there, incessant, biological,
         seeking a way in. They push and gather
at every pore, but the flesh is sealed—
         His doing.
Soaking in his vat of embalming fluid, Lenin looks restful,
         meditative, a high official in his bath
in his dacha, far away
         from the controlled air of the mausoleum . . .

Characteristic is the massive weight of both passages, so unlike the pecu-
liarly substanceless mass of much contemporary poetry, the mass of the reiterated
indeterminate. Nor is this the inquiring, elastic capaciousness of the note-taker,
the generous gatherer. Rather this is mass as dense accrual of detail around par-
ticular ideas, ideas sufficiently magnetic or profound to allow detail to adhere
in varied ways.

If the shape and manner of these poems owe something to Whitman, the temperament is less affable, its luminous, mortal, ecstatic reach closer (among Americans) to Crane. But scale here is less purely expansive, more corrective: Levin's animating fury goes back deeper into our linguistic and philosophic history: to Blake's tyger, to the iron judgments of the Old Testament.

Her syntactical signatures are two. If syntax reveals, more deeply than any other formal element, the style of a poet's thought, then Levin's art owes most to, is closest to, these earliest masters. (Though it is also true that readers can only hear echoes of what they themselves have read.) But surely there is something of Blake in Levin's driving imperatives and urgent repeated questions, and something of the biblical in her savage moral intensity:

> oh doctor, angel, person healed,
>> do you think this is grandeur, to see myself
> as an avatar of healing,
>> to see in the sick child the fever of the world,
> and to say to the people in the distant air
>> circling and circling, like planets caught,
> the fires of their own
>> history's wreckage, Come down
> into the burning,
>> feel it,

> so you can not live it anymore.

Such questions and imperatives make up a syntax of insistence; its proliferating clauses, animated by a need to refine, to amplify, crucial perception, have nothing in common with ornament. This is the language of the prophet: Levin's art, in this book certainly, takes place in a kind of mutating day of judgment: it means to wipe a film from our eyes. It is a dare, a challenge, and, for all its considerable beauty, the opposite of the seductive. How remote this art is, in its scale and seriousness, from most of what surrounds it, from what could be called the ambitious minor, with its polished self consciousness: on one end, the depressingly flawless small lyric, and on the other, facile amplitude, its very pointlessness promoted into philosophical exploration.

Also at odds with contemporary habit is Levin's refusal to identify herself by gender. She writes sometimes as a woman, sometimes as a man (often simply as a human soul):

> —this green
> brightness—
>> like a stage lit up in a ring of dark trees, where he has come
> with a stick of birch, where he has come
>> to not have a body—

And later, in the same incandescent poem:

> He knows the names, from his brother's textbook,
> *calyx, lepidoptera, labia, clitoris,* he'd thought
>> they were beautiful,
> as he spreads the pictures down on the ground, his eyes slow
>> as a tracing finger, he's a boy,
> he will have this body,
>> what will he do now with the beautiful names.

Current American literary life being what it is, a well documented and scrutinized arena (the audience made up almost entirely of practitioners), a lit trail from the MFA programs through the multiple journals, it is rare to encounter so substantially, and for the first time, so mature a gift. Formed, complex, learned: but where was it through those nervous earlier stages, when we would normally have been watching it, speculating about it, ministering and judging?

It was an extraordinary experience for me, to discover this talent entire, in a book. Nor can excerpts give any sense of its scope, its music, the poems' tidal power:

> To say, I hurt—
> To say, The heavens are empty—
> To say I hurt, the heavens are empty, the streets are empty,
>> beer cans scatter, the click and tink of their tinny bells—

To say there is a Dark Age grasping for light, extending its bent
    hands back to the other one, which had striven and striven,
while this one doesn't even know
    it strives—

And to say, The sirens are advancing.
And to say, It's 1999.
And to say, My gas bill is late.
And to say, There is no lover.

    And to rise up to the stove and pour the water in the cup,
to watch the tea stain it,
    while mercury opens his doctoring wings and hovers
at the edge of the ceiling,
    to cocoon you,
to give you a stage—

Sensuous, compassionate, violent, extravagant: what an amazing debut this is,
a book of terrors and marvels.

BODY

The way of compassion,
in which the knights of our lord
travel by night and by day,
in the darkness of the body
and in the soul's light.

[*The Quest of the Holy Grail*]

LENIN'S BATH

The future of the body—that's a purely political question.

—DR. SERGEI S. DEBOV

The assistants lift him gently,
gently. For a moment, the one lifting under his arms
        is in the attitude of an artistic
sorrow—It is
        the Deposition, the taking down of the god.
But then one of them wraps his limp body around him
        like a coat,
marches around to the laughter, saying
        "Comrades, comrades—" He is dead, he is so dead
he is nothing, he is a cloth to tend.
        When Debov walks in, disheveled, yawning, the assistants
are all business, filling the vat
        with the secret fluid
that makes him supple, that makes him clean.
        They are so tender,
lowering him into the tub. Their gloved hands come away
        fleshy pink.

        When they've gone, Debov sits watching. He imagines
the sheath of bacteria he knows is there, incessant, biological,
        seeking a way in. They push and gather
at every pore, but the flesh is sealed—
        His doing.
Soaking in his vat of embalming fluid, Lenin looks restful,
        meditative, a high official in his bath
in his dacha, far away
        from the controlled air of the mausoleum,
the schoolchildren filing past him
        unblinking, the veterans who stand, expressionless.
Debov watches

as the germs crawl up and down the length
of the body, scouring, sniffing
        for that open hole—The cold windows in the laboratory
condense with his breath, and the flies lie hungry
        in the snow.

EYELESS BABY

Your face is smashed.
It's a pot thrown down.
    You're mashed against a window no one can see,
not even you,
    with your red wounds for eyes—
I'm looking

    at the teeth in the gum under the lip that isn't there,
but I can't find your eyes, they're lost
    in your head,
your nose a single nostril,
    your whole palate cleft
from the bolt of being born, and now you're

    arching your back,
lifting your belly, and I can see the lightning
    coming out of your body,
I can see the fire, the red pools in your sockets,
    the combusted seeds of an enormous
light—
    Can I

crawl in them, look through them, I am so sure they're a door,
    if I pried into the fused lids I would find
ice, stars, space with its cold fires spreading out
    beyond the body,
if I could just shimmy through them,
    I would see what's inside us:
the muteness,
    the blindness—

because I don't know what it's like to be born
    without tears,
because sighted I am blind to all
    that's invisible,
because without eyes I imagine
    anything:

gems, suns, whatever conducts the light.

I'm seeing this
through Richard's eyes.
        The dark warehouse, the lights, the card to get in.
The floor shiny with moisture, stains on the walls,
        eggwhite, yellow,
the room sodden with cock-smell, excess,
        want.
Sweat pours from the men as they smack and kiss
        into each other, fucking themselves
out of suit and tie, lies
        to the parents, the boss, the wife —
Spread out on mats, in doorless rooms, calling
        "Fuck me! I want to be fucked!"
                        Don't you want to say this
every day of your life?
        In the airshaft of your apartment building,
in the cubicles of your office?
        Hoses to wash out the shit and blood.
To be clean for the fucking, to be clean
        for the love.
                        But can you see them? See the organisms
stretching their tendrils?
        Into the cracks in the rectum, into the blood sluicing
through the bodies on the floor?
        The building's a hothouse, a breeder, a nest —
Feel the steam, the musk, how you stew unknowing
        in a petri dish, sowing the seed
into the ass in front of you, grinding, grinding
        for love?

(7)

Who rent the sky? What cracked open
        to let this in?
God with his beaker standing over the roof,
        pouring, pouring—
This is the experiment, the laboratories haphazard
        in the trick's hotel room, the used
syringe.
        Do you think it is the scourge, do you think
you are the chosen?
        It will spread, it will spread.
Into the backs of cars behind the football field,
        into the master bedroom
in the suburbs.
        Can you feel yourself wanting, can you feel the love?
Angels gather in the corners of the building.
        They do not judge.

BODY OF MAGNESIA

When the door between the worlds opened
I ceased to be a ghost, I became
the blood in my fingers in the veins of my hands
I felt the world under my feet
with its nails and its splinters I felt
the salt the red water in the loam of my chest I was

no longer a ghost, the vapors were gone,
I was solid, I hurt, my wings could be broken,
it was joy, I was living in it,
I bled, I cried.

The broken teeth, the ulcers, eating into the backs
of people
        who have spent years sitting in chairs, in the green tiled halls
of a hospital,
        trying to find a place to read,
to think,
        to find, like Faye, a place to turn one's back and cry,
to say, like Faye,
        When I cry I know it is Jesus crying, because Jesus
is in my chest, he's crying
        for me, for my cut-off legs, he's crying

        for you Paul, your feet bent like his, your bones stuck like nails
through the flesh of your body,
        pinning you to a wheelchair for twenty-three years,
your hands shaped like claws,
        skin-hard,
tremoring, your shirt covered
        with egg yolk and coffee,
your green pants stained with pus and shit—
        and the doctors,

        gliding by you like sails, saying
Hello, Hello,
        as you open the stink of your plaque-caked mouth and say
Hello, you are beautiful,
        your soft eyes, your old man smell,
the way you stick out your clawed hand to shake mine and say
        Thank you,

popping chocolate in your mouth when we shared
      Easter candy,
the dull brown saliva falling in torrents because you couldn't
      stop talking about poetry Paul

      I see you in a wheelchair,
on the weedstrewn windswept eastside
      of the island, the Pepsi sign curling over the banks
of Queens, the clouds rolling black
      in from the Hudson, and you are saying Yes, now,
I am giving myself up to the wind,
      I am a kite, I am a bird, I am weightless and beyond gravity,
slipping up and diffusing,
      the million captive particles of me
falling like mist over the hospital,
      because I am wholly mind,
wholly air,
      I am dropping these wrecked bone shackles—

THE NURSE

There are so many now, perched on the headboard, opening and closing
    their wings like moths. The kidney
is failing, and so many are arriving, alighting on the blanket, the pillow,
    falling around
the comatose patient, settling in drifts against the paper gown.
    You've been seeing this,
you've been watching them gather, you've told no one how the buzzing
    keeps growing
around the bed. Now they crowd like a sea around the body,
    listing and pushing,
the pulse of their wings lifting the current, you can feel it,
    the wind,
on the hairs of your arms, making the lamp sway,
    ruffling the chart
at the foot of the bed, they are hanging from tubes,
    perched on the monitor,
pressing and pressing with a rising hum, you can hear it,
    the whirring,
the din of their waiting, as they rustle and jostle
    and launch with a roar,
a roar of angels swarming over the body, burrowing headfirst
    into every pore—

THE BABY ON THE TABLE

     Everything is so dark under the baby, the table
floats legless,
     a rectangle of light. Around it
the angels are bending their doctoral faces,
     the baby unswaddled,
undisturbed.
     See the kliegs
bearing down on it, throwing up a stark light
     on the angels' faces, Mary seeping in
to the black floor, dress vanishing
     in its deepening
folds—
     She is a head, a moon, floating without expression
above her naked child,
     the distance between them filling with ready,
angels bending closer in a luminous cone—
     Will they do it? Will they dip their hands
into the light?
     Will they fish out its heart, its lungs, its soul
like an aspirin, lifting it bloodless
     from the milky white?
Must there come a time, a line, a moment, a stanza
     where I say

On February 9th, 1965 I was slit through the belly
     without anesthetic
to remove a gangrenous ileum? To make you look
     in the sterile bucket at the side
of the gurney,

at the blackened, pussed and stinking intestine,
to tap your shoulder and look in your face asking
        Is that you? Is that you?
Have you ever been hurt, have you ever been cut, is it only
        physical knives?
Is this how I write about
        the baby on the table? By looking at a
poor black and white print of a nameless Adoration
        by the School of Jan-Stephan Von Calcar?
The print is so poor, is that an egg, a star
        through the trees in the distance,
are they sheep, are they men,
        kneeling under its light? I can't tell
if they are bending in lamentation or praising
        halleluyah, if the egg
is a cross
        in a circle of light—when will they lower

the kiss, the fist, the sharpened
        scalpel, the angels
are waiting, calm, impassive, the emanations
        of science
in each white face—
        Can you help me sew up
what they're about to open? Can you feel
        the chill of the table
on your own small back?
        I keep looking at the baby again and again,
outlined on the table by a membrane
        of shadow,
how it looks up at the sky unconcerned—Where
        is the fault
in this studied composure? Where is the crack in the gloss
        over suffering,

is it here, at the base, where the paint is chipping,
      revealing the starkness beneath? Look in there,
in the fissures between
      the blackened oils, and see the form
of your very own cross,
      slipping through the vent in the hospital nursery
and alighting on your chest your chosen
      star,
marking you for the scalpels of light.

IN THE SURGICAL THEATRE

In the moment between
the old heart and the new
two angels gather at the empty chest.

The doctors flow over them as winds, as blurs, unnoticed but as currents
around this body, the flesh of the chest peeled back
as petals, revealing

a hole.
In it

the layers are fluttering—the back muscle, the bone, the chrome
    of the table,
the tiled floor with its spatters of blood—

—fluttering as veils over the solid,
        fluttering—

The angels, gathering. Small, and untroubled, perched quietly
    on the rib cage, its cupped hands trying
to keep in.
    Around them the hands of the doctors,
hurrying—white flaps,
    white wings—
the clicks and whirrs of the lung machine . . .

Do you want it to be stars, do you want it to be a hole to heaven,
    clean and round—

Do you want their hands, dipping and dipping, flesh sticking like jelly
     to the tips of their gloves—

Hovering at the edge of this
     spot-lit stage,
loathe to enter, loathe to leave, is it terror,
     fascination,
the angels too occupied to turn their gaze to you?
     Go down,

go in.
     The angels perch on either side of the hole like handles
round a grail.
     The bleeding tissues part, underneath the solid shimmers
black, like a pool.
     The lights above the table enter and extinguish,
the light of your face

     enters,
is extinguished,
     is this why you've come? The frigid cauldron
that is life without a heart?
     I know,
I'm tired of the battle too, the visible and invisible clashing together,
     the hands with the scalpels

flashing and glinting like flags and standards,
     fighting,
fighting to the death—
     When they cut you down the middle you fled.
The angels descended.
     You came up here with me,
with the voiceless

thousands at the edge of the curtain, hearts beating
with ambivalence.
      Do you know if you want it? Is that jumble of spit and bone
so worth it
      that you would go down again and be
a body
      raging with loss, each beat of the heart

like the strike of a hammer,
      spiking the nails in, to feel, to *feel*—
I learned this from you, Father, all my life
      I've felt your resign to the hurt
of living,
      so I came up here, to the scaffolding above
the surgical theatre

      to watch you decide.
Can you go on with this mortal vision? To the sword rearing up now
      in orange fire, the angels turning
to face you poised at the hole's
      brink, their eyes in flames, in sprays of blood
their wings beating
      against the steel wedge prying open the rib cage, is it

      for you? Are they protecting
you?

      But you bend down, you look in, you dip in
a finger, Father,
      you bring it to your mouth and you taste it,
and I can feel the cold that is black on my tongue, it is bitter,
      it is numbing,
snuffing the heart out, the heat,
      the light,
and when will they lift the new heart like a lamp—

and will you wait—

the doctors pausing with their knives uplifted, the rush of wings
stirring a wind—

Personal History

per fretum febris

I
(like lifting a curtain)

Magic chest.
        Open it up.
See the baby inside?
        The tubes twisting out of the wrists and ankles,
trickles of blood where the needles go in—
        Soft machines inhale, exhale.
The plasma bag, dripping the minutes.
        Moisture beading on the rim of the glass.

The drip-bags hang, heavy as flowers,
        droplets collecting like dew, like time—
The body's a fruit, the baby's inside it,
        ripening in its own
steam—
        Follow the yellow food
flowing in like water,
        bruises flowering

round the entering tubes—
        Reach in.
With your latexed hands through the humid air, and lift
        the skin
over the belly,
        where the intestines coil
in the brackish water,
        rot running through it a blooded
green—

The rotting wood, the moss.
Dripping luminous to the jungle floor, a fever
    of banana
decay—
    Planes.
Orange smoke billowing from the napalmed river, flaming slowly
    to the sea—

The plasma bag, bleeding the minutes.

II

If you'd listened to me before you'd know what I was saying.
You'd know that I was saying

the upraised scalpel, a glint in the light.

The upraised scalpel, the brush of a wing, invisible.

Because I have this compulsion, to lift the shirt over my distended belly,
to show you the scars.

Like a revealed religion, the cross, the x, slicing into the skin,
Ave doctorus, Ave angelus, white caps floating like wings on the air—

Reach in.

Do you expect to find light?
    Here,
in this windowless room, digging your thumb

deeper and deeper into the hospital nursery,
    to the dark stink
in the bowels —
    It's 1965, the world's
radiating out of it,
    the tubes like spokes of a living wheel —
And are you connected?
    Pale face hovering

over the incubator glass,
    pale moon
through the lactic trees, boots tensing
    in the milk-green mud, footprints,
feet,
    swallowed —
It was the doctors, their scalpels, like steel-green angels,
    arcing the knife that could cut the rot

out of miles of river snaked by the silent Viet Cong,
    boys in rags
up to their necks in the malarial water,
    holding their guns up,
high —
    Don't you see, how every time I look
between the scalpelled flaps, pinned back
    to the sides of the belly, it's a war

rotting inside? Is this
    why it's important to tell you, how the baby lay strapped

with its belly sliced open,
        doctors plunging their hands in
at six days old, to remove
        a gangrenous
ileum?
        And the boys croaking

"Don't take my leg Doc, don't take my leg—"
        and the boys with their intestines
sprung out in loops,
        Mr. Johnson's can of snakes—
For so long I thought
        surgical white
was the color of the soul, I've been floating
        for years

in the albanic air round the hospital nursery,
        above the orange smoke billowing
from the napalmed river,
        huts collapsed
into palm fronds and fire, and the people
        staggering away
to lie burned and bleeding in the soft-haired ferns
        curling

round the incubator glass—

                    IV

Is this
        how I can tell it? How it
can make sense?

        By placing it
in history?

Doctor—

Do you know what it's like to be
         connected? As flesh to machine? To be fed
not by the nipple but by the needle cutting
         into the veins of the ankle?
To never be handled by a bare hand, to never
         look in a face that is not masked, to never feel air
not enclosed by a box,
         and don't we live this way every day, gloved and masked and dying,
                 I'm

trying to figure out why it's important to show you, because I have this
                 compulsion
to rip the shirt from my distended belly and show you the scars—

like the botched job of a drunken butcher, x-ing jerkily into the skin,
do you know what I am saying?

Nurses swoop and hover, cold birds in the tropical air.

                          v

In the sick world
         on the sick day
on which I was born, sick and dying, rotting
         tuber
in a glass—
         Was there someone
trying to heal himself, sutured,
         dreaming,

tears?
      That person
is the guiding angel, lifting now
      over the stucco roofs
of the white hospital
      where I was born, having hovered there
for so very long
      while the ghost of me kept burning in the glass—

Unstitch
      my deepest scar, and find the baby
on the cold chrome table,
      descend through that ravine of bleeding flesh and look up
at the people
      circling like gulls in the humid air:
the medics, the nurses, the mothers and fathers, generals and presidents,
      hovering above the stink of ripeness and death,

if you looked inside them would there be
      suffering,
the capacity or desire to heal
      through suffering,
if you took the scalpel and opened them up
      would there be the baby,
vital,
      inside?

I want to see it,
      arriving now out of the blood-rich sky,
fat and shining,
      as if the healing were not from the outside in,
as if the world were sick and the tubes
      radiating out in a corona of ribbons, of fiery light,
carried all life's innocence
      through the sickness of the world,

oh doctor, angel, person healed,
      do you think this is grandeur, to see myself
as an avatar of healing,
      to see in the sick child the fever of the world,
and to say to the people in the distant air
      circling and circling, like planets caught,
the fires of their own
      history's wreckage, Come down
into the burning,
      feel it,

so you can not live it anymore.

H O M E

The heart, being full of blood, casts a shadow.

[*Gray's Anatomy*]

FIELD

The antelope white against the charred hills
     eaten by fire,
the golden trees, the upstairs window,
     something

is running across the field,
     can you see it coming
through the yellow grass, can you see it coming
     from the windowpane,
are you closing the shutters, do you think it is rain?

     The wind banging the shutters back, the antelope,
the golden trees, the skirt of your dress
     caught on the wire, the trampled grass,
the barbed fence, something

     is running over the field,
do you think it is crows, do you think it is dust,
     are you huddled
under the window frame, are your legs cold,
     are your eyes shut?

Something is running across the field—
     The wind hurling the shutters back—
The antelope, the charred hills. The yellow trees,
     the parted field.

SILO

Silo. The yellow waving.
  See the hay-musted window
with the broken panes.
  They are punched out, all of them,
was it your hand?
  The sheep are at the fence with their faces up at you,
the yellow grass swaying
  blade after blade—you're watching

the jagged glass glinting
  in the static sun, the one blue shard thin
as a needle,
  sticking out from the frame like a gift to you—
Will you be pricked? Will you awake?
  And move from this place
where the silo dwarfs you, the years inside

  its tyrannous shadow, telling you that this
is your truest face:
  a smudge refracted twelve times
in the shattered panes—
  If you went to the glass would there be
a feeling?
  If you slid the edge down your thumb would you know
you were touched?

  You can hear the shattering over and over,
the bloodied fist coming
  again and again,

and you remember you were mad, mad
     at all of them,
rising like behemoths out of the field,
     throwing towers of shadow on your confused little form —

the shards digging into your knuckles like sand.

WIND

My house was a house of winds
and my father was of the wind
and we were of the earth

and we were torn by him,
we were stripped by him,
by the bellows of his body,

by the twisting of his voice
coming shaking, elemental, before the kitchen table
where we sat like stones and he stood

like a hammer over the rocks
of our faces, and threw down the glasses
and threw down the plates, the hail of him

scattering across the tiled floor
as he whirled in his fury out the back door,
slamming into the air—

He was gone, he was gone
and the storm was coming, I could hear it
on the radio crackling in the kitchen

as we ran out the door and headed
for the cellar, the dirty wind gusting
and stinging our eyes as my mother

bent down and hurried with the lock—
When she opened the cellar doors
I thought I saw him coming, the grass

bowing down, bowing down, bowed flat
by the black clouds bearing down
like fists, so I ran out to the field

and opened my arms, the flayed skin of my coat
rippling behind me, the voice of my sister
calling my name, as I streamed out like a flag

into the currents and felt the wind slam
into all of my sockets, and stood like a stick
and was whittled to pieces,

flying off with the twigs
that kept pelting my face —
I was in the air

but in the arms of my mother,
clutching me and running us back
towards the cellar, and I held her, looking back

and saw the tornado twisting down from the sky,
coming for us as we ran on the earth,
and I stretched out my arms because I wanted

to touch it, I stretched out my arms
because I wanted to fly with the fence-posts
in that furious rapture —

And then we were in the cellar,
in the darkness with the jam jars,
while he roared and tore past our doors.

Mother holds you by a leash.
You're babbling, incoherent, spit
bobbing from your chin.
She is calm, her eyes are slits, they say
    There is nothing wrong,
     this is nothing different.
You've been knocked senseless, you've always been,
it's just that it's been covered
by your tie pins and cufflinks,
her with her hands folded deep in her sleeves—
it's a family secret.
The two of you on the sidewalk, welcoming me in
past the tulips withering in the desert heat.
You're straining at the collar,
the sagging face of an idiot
struck dumb by grief—
Mother smiles imperceptibly,
she's got a good grip.
I'm so disgusted I don't greet you

but walk down a narrow hallway in a coal-blackened house,
walls covered with soot and baroque design—
to find the two of you facing each other
at antique wood desks,
doing your separate checkbooks
by the candle's dim light.
This is the ruse, the moneyed palliative,
that stuffs your mania in Mother's
pocket, the gilded scale between you
weighing the expense—

So you can say: I never tore the back door off its hinge.
    I never smashed the chair
    under which you cowered.

CHILL CORE

Are you becoming enslaved
    to a bad idea? That it all
just *happened*
    like wind or sky,
that there was nothing human in it—it was just
    part of the elements, an abuse
cosmic
    in its inevitable rounds—

I know, they were like lights, the moon bitter and the sun furious
    in a single sky,
you the dumb substance
    lodged in the alfalfa waving in acres,
bound to the rage,
    the shriveling light—
Can you see that you're not there anymore?
    You're here,

in this dream, at the shore of a vast and slow-petalled sea,
    the top of your skull perched
on your open palm—
    The wind is moving
through the convolutions, a frost dusting
    the gray ridges
of your open brain, glinting in the frigid
    light—

The white question is opening
    in your left hand,
the bone you can dig with, that can upend

the memory
of being human
      locked in the brain's chill core—
that being of grief and terror
      I will help you assemble here.

Wind. I can feel it
brushing up the hair on my bare arms.
Sorry. I'm sorry. Lying here with my eyes closed,
book face down on the rise of my belly.
Do you think I'm asleep?
I can feel you watching me, I'm not asleep.
Feel how soft the steady wind is, the one fruitless plum
    left still standing,
spades of shade flickering
on the dry grass where you sit,
watching me with expressionless eyes—
Listen. Do you hear the chimes? The wind
clanging their sorries together
under the striped shadows of the over-hang, all their sorries
ringing round us sorry sorry I want to say
    I'm sorry
for my bare feet on the kitchen floor,
barbecue tongs in my hand and screaming but why
should I say I'm sorry, you never
comforted, commiserated, solaced me, sitting there
with your face in a book while your mother served
an insult of a dinner—*He*
    never said he was sorry
for hemorrhaging to death at fifty-four and leaving me
with my mother's sharp tongue honed
to a skewer, and not another single man in the house—
Sorry? Did you say Sorry? Do you think I'm dickless,
standing here ringed by you, your mother, your sisters, your aunts,
that I need the cluck and cloy of your sorry?

Did you hope I was a myth, that I wasn't a monster,
        that it was all, merely, psychological?

When I rise up like a beast because the steak isn't cooked right,
when I smash the platter with my fist and scream
at your mother, blood-juice dripping from my hand—
Do you think my father's tumor has bloomed in me yet?
I'm not sick. I'm not dying.

Hot.
        Motionless at the window.
Forehead beaded with a line of fevered moons, swelling
        and then dropping
to the floor—
        Parched.
Face flushed. Room flushed, red shadows licking up the walls,
        the ceiling,
you briared in it like a rose on a spit, rubiate,
        carnadine—
Breathing.
        With your mouth half open,
staring into the cool of the glass—Look
        in the window as a mirror, and see
your shadow
        jerking behind you, puppet,
spider,
        up the orange-blood walls—
Listen.
        Hear the restless hiss-whisper, there in the belly
 of the big black stove, fire beasties
        speaking up to you—
Asking

        Is this
your oven fairy tale?
        Cabin on a hill a shifting house of fever, door locked
by a heavy wooden bar
        somebody put

on the outside—And outside
    the snow.
Outside
    the white flinging itself in bits on the white,
no hills anymore,
    the sheep at the fence that have black faces
beacons
    blinking through the ice—

And inside the fire.
    Water glass sweating on the hearth—
Inside the thermometer in its plastic case
    saying there's not a damn thing wrong with you—
Can't you see that this house is your head, you at the front window
    like the pupil of an eye,
armless, legless, unable to move?
    And if your fever broke—
And if you were healed—
    Up in the morning, sweat
crusted on your brow, to see the miles covered
    in mirrored shingles of snow,
the sun at the end of them
    rising, rising—

All around you the walls are flickering, aces, tongues, hissing,
    flickering,
out of the belly of the enormous wood stove—
    Will you climb in it?
Will you be your own
    homunculus,
burning away the detritus of years
    of living so long in this house?

    You must do it. You must.

Crushed mouse head on the picnic table—
    it is your thumb,
your tongue.
    Some part of you
hanging from the great owl's mouth—
    What were you thinking when you took shelter here,
standing in a gray
    powder of droppings, tumors
of matted hair and bone
    rotting the floor of this abandoned barn—
Imagine,
    the crush and the blood. The live
feast
    up in the eaves, the enormous, rotting nest—

You thought it was him, you thought it was all
    him,
turning toward the hills where the hares were running,
    their yellow coats gleaming like suns in the snow,
visible,
    takeable,
fleeing
    the sharp-cocked claw—
And now you feel them,
    under your feet: the broken shells that are hers—

The great swoop and then you, little mouse,
    pinched up
by the skin of your nape,
    hovering above the white-streaked floor—

And that you wanted it, the dark fold of embrace,
     cradling you away
from the arctic wind
     whipping through these cankered walls—
The dark well
     of her open eye,
the beak, the lunge, the eating.

A tendon, an eye. Hanging
    from a string of fat, steaming
in the morning light, the beak, the pincers,
    holding it tight.
Do you think it's repulsive? Do you think it is
    an amber jewel?
Black bird, white bird, unconcerned with you—
    See it hop, pick
through the frosted fur, the blood
    thawing, beginning to run—Magpie, treasure
in the mangled deer.
    Claws biting in
as it cocks its head at you,
    eye swinging from its mouth like a diamond
tear,
    cold and glittering in the icy air—asking
Do you think
    these feathers are beautiful, spread out
iridescent
    against this matted haunch? Will you be like this
with the bones of your father,
    will you radiate
a vital plumage
    and perch on him in the frozen ditch?
No pause, no grief, the heart beating
    in you—
a red scrap of flesh in your black beak.

HIVE

Whirring.
    The tall grass shifts.
Crouch there, part through it—what do you see?
    The gold bees weaving,
braiding the air;
    the sugared drip uncurling
down the hard gray oak—
    For deer.
For bear.
    Sniff—the bees are weaving;
can you see the hive?
    You can feel

the hexagons opening in the golden light, the bees
    sticky with honey
as they sun on the branches, there are hundreds,
    their wings
too sweet-drenched to fly, and are you
    rising—both eyes trained
on the ambered bark—
    will you stand two-legged and cut
through the grasses,
    will you take your stick
and strike down hive?
    Step through, step through,

and see that it's you,
    arms strapped to the ashen
branches,
    your chest burst open by an enormous grief—

The bees are weaving, bright, industrious, in and out
        of the claws
of the rib cage, honey crusting on your heaving
        ribs—
can you be alive in so much sweetness,
        breasts hanging on skin hinges
around the yellow hive?
        Can you crawl out of asking

the origin of sorrow, now, through the grass,
        in the animal moment,
will you nuzzle the roots in search
        of the combs,
the resin like jewels in the burnished
        light?
Climb up, part
        your shattered chest like a veil, and lick
at the honey
        welling over your bones—
It has nothing to do with your happiness,
        or grief.

D O O R

And then an uprush of air—
And then the cellar doors
    banging back,
the strong dusk light falling in
    like a stanchion,
a gold nail hammered through the blackened trees—
    Can you see it? You, psyche, burden,
friend?
    This is the first time I can speak, the first time
I've seen you
    recede from the front in a fission of mist, the doors of this keep
flying open in the auric light—
    And I can smell

the green smell of straw
    puddled in urine, the musk of fur
coming up from the hutches, laid out in a row in the leaning
    light,
the blood smell of rust
    in the hinges of these open doors—
I want to look

    in the black deep and the golden light, if I had two faces
and could stand, always, at
    the distinction, on the wooden step
between the gold shaft and the cellar
    beneath me,
I could be like the eye in the center of my head—always to see and
    never to enter, never to feel
the light pierce and the darkness snuff it,

the darkness down and the light
pierce it,
the exhausting round of wounding and healing, I don't want
to feel, but can't bear
not feeling

the light swift through the cottonwood leaves, their edges enflamed
but their bodies
in shadow, black spades oranged
in the orange-gold light—
I don't know how
to get out of this beauty, I was shut up so long
in darkness and weeping,
but here
the rabbits are black stones on fire in the grass, hurt
because they're lit, hurt
because they're burning, as if the light is leaving
thumbs of fire

on their curling bodies, on my feet as I stand
between the sun and the cellar,
can you tell me if this
is the place I must enter, to burn without consumption
in the ice-fired night?
Will I burn from the inside out like a star,
will I burn from the outside in
in wood-fire,
is it blaze,
is it anguish,
to be the conscious sun that does not die,
for isn't life fire, living the human burning torch—

And then a slight wind like a pointing finger,
lifting toward the flame-struck field.

The Beautiful Names

for Tim Stotz

Dark shaft.

    The milky pearl.

At the top of the milkweed, pod
    about to unfold.

Stalk erect in the shadow of the pines, sliver of light
    burning through like a finger,
probing it,
    that droplet
at the tip of the pod,
    moist,
white,
    dew—

And the gravelly paths lined with them, on either side,
    cattails
like a stand of scepters through which the boy comes running,
    panting for air
by the autoshop and abandoned garage, house
    burned
to its foundations—

    Away.

From the brother waving his dick around, saying *Look, see it?*
    dark of the closed shared room—

    Away.

To the cool eden, electric green of moss on rock,
       iris at the cold clear stream —

He's twelve.
       His brother's a bully, pinning him to the wall
until he can't breathe,
       rubbing the wet-dreamed sheets in his face — saying
This is what it is to be a man, butthole,
       do you think you're a man?

       This is what it is.

                              *

       The brother, coaxing his straining cock along, dark shaft for the
              milky pearl.

       The father, blustering into the house like air, vanishing —

       The mother who clings, who will not let him cling —

       Heat of the closed shared room.

       But the iris, above the orange lichen, bending to the cold clear
              stream —

       Bud unfolding, wasp crawling in and then out again,
the yellow sugar,
       and the wasp buzzing away and the flower still standing,
stalk unbroken by love —

       And that was love,
wasn't it?
       But how could he be sure, unmarked as it was by words or blows,
his brother's fist,

his classmates snickering,
dirty words for dirty girls in a huddle at the edge of the soccer field—

Yellow in the tongue's blue flame.

A sudden flush, suffusing his cheeks.

∗

But who put the box at the foot of the pine.

Festooned with fur, a green procreation
of moss and mold
        at its conventional edges, split at one seam from the weight
of the first fall rains—

the moist white dew—

which he does not see,
as he makes his way through the raspberry bracken, to the small pond
        where he can not have a body,
where he can be
        breath on the water—

press of the closed shared room.

The morning's failure, nature's failure, the cool of the ferns
with their seductive hairs,
        like Robyn's hair, like Celia's hair, all the girls he knows
flitting through his head like butterflies, he's twelve, he can't

be rid of it—

until the green light falling—

the dragonfly skimming and leaving its Z
shimmering—

    wink of gems in its vanishing trail, diamonds small
as the heads of pins,
      this glade and pond—this green
brightness—
      like a stage lit up in a ring of dark trees, where he has come
with a stick of birch, where he has come
      to not have a body—

    and the split box sagging at the foot of the pine.

    Which he sees now,
wet black letters under a rim of moss,
      to which he bends
with a probing finger, he's a boy, he will not
      be rid of it—

    so the cardboard splits:

    so he pulls it open:

    wet magazines stacked like cards, his pick, his flesh
fortune—

    and he lifts one, pulls up a sticky page,
and thighs without torsos, breasts without faces, in a wheel of burgundy,
      dusk and rose, how

    can he not have a body—

    here in the green close world—

this burlesque of flesh called *Easy Woman*,
Sopping Object,
    Ridicule, Honey, Soft Box for the thumb to plumb through, how
can he be rid of it—

    He knows the names, from his brother's textbook,
calyx, lepidoptera, labia, clitoris, he'd thought
      they were beautiful,
as he spreads the pictures down on the ground, his eyes slow
      as a tracing finger, he's a boy,
he will have this body,
      what will he do now with the beautiful names.

WORLD

The darkness held the brightness and the spark of light in thrall.

[*Hippolytus*]

SMOKE

The schoolhouse is red, as it's supposed to be.
And the smell of woodsmoke, like a fire, like a fire.
Where are we going, my nation my loved one,
in this valley like a sink with no drain at the bottom
where you and I trudge through the snow.

Where are we going, my nation my loved one,
in this pit of water where we'll drown come Spring,
in this poem without instruction,
without point or moral,
where the smoke stands in for the flame.

POWER

He was standing with his dog, his great big German Shepherd, he kept it
    tight on its leash,
so it was always straining, so it had the appearance of stealth, of being
    at bay—
how he loved to tug on its chain.

Not a leather strap, no, but a great iron collar, and a leash of steel links
    wrapped twice round the meat of his hand—
tugging it, the chain, the panting dog, which sniffed at nothing
    but strained or sat,
its great tongue lolling, its yellow teeth sharp with a bone gleam—

And when the other dog-walker came strolling by, over the hot sidewalk
    outside of the bank,
he made the dog sit and listened to it growl, murmuring You want it,
    I know,
you want to *get it*, don't you, the whisper a caress all down the black

flank, rippling with tension as the growl erupted, as the man chuckled,
    pulling the chain,
the dog up now, straining and snapping at the bright summer air,
    trying to tear its own spit
to shreds—

And then the man said DOWN! and the dog instantly cowered,
    settled itself
to the bare ground beside him, panting and swallowing like before.
    The man stroked and stroked
its big black head, cooing Yes baby, I know, I know it, yes—
    loving it, its brutality, and obedience.

MARVELOUS FATHER

Slobodan Milosovic is a marvelous father.
He takes his children to the zoo every Sunday.
He turns his back on the snipers up in the hills
so his daughter can laugh at the little brown monkeys.
This is what we must strive for,
O friends, O villagers,
to be a zoo in the heart of a bombed-out city,
to be the whim of a girl with her hand on the gun,
the gun that is the man Radovan Karadzic,
the gun that is the man Franjo Tudjman,
the gun that is the hand named Hitler and Stalin,
devil twins of terror of 1945.
This is what we must strive for,
to be the snipers asleep above the insomniac town,
to be, every one of us, marvelous fathers,
to throw our children in the tanks as we splatter their enemies,
to throw our women in the wells — so what if they drown!
We must do it, do it, again and again
to the whores that are the wives of Slobodan Milosovic
who killed our chickens and our cows and drank all our vodka
O brothers, O friends!
This is what we must strive for!
To be the horsemen of plagues in the homes of the criminals,
to crush them like hawks and that lackey Mussolini,
to strafe them and bomb them like an American fist,
to be like MacArthur, like Lenin, like the Kaiser,
like Dracul the blood-eater with his stakes and his slaughter,
like your father, Haris, and *your* father, Marko —

We know they are such marvelous men.

FIRST CRADLE

I have been fighting against myself.

— PARZIVAL

I

Sound stops. The grenades arc down slowly.
You are beatific, standing white
in the leaden smoke
coiling from the charnel on the ground:
a child, a goat, one limb
fused into another,
hoofed ember glowing on the human bone—
The limbless hundreds. Watching you
from the roofless hospital, your voluminous
white
gown.
The grenades

stop.
They do not touch down. The bullets hang
in crooked rows in the air, rungs to the unclouded
sky—is this
you? The bright flame of you
knowing better
blazing in to the clouded mind?
What I wanted to do

was parachute in
to the war-torn country, the light shining round me
an auric
shield—
To feel the bullet
between my thumb and forefinger, hot and trembling,

                a metallic
fly—
        As if in my total consciousness
I could reach out and pluck it
        from the sulfurous air, saving
the huddled

        mark—
How did I get here?
        I was somewhere on a turnpike
between Boston and New York, listening to a history of the Bosnian war,

        when I saw myself descend.
Diamond shield in the mud-slogged trench, thicket
        of severed legs.
I touched them: I wanted them whole. I touched them: would they
        reanimate,
my own white hands smeared
        with their jelly
as I set them standing again? What was this
        foundation I was building,
the smell of brine
        crusted on metal, blood
the first cradle of war,
        there in the ditch with the hospital carnage,
the two legs standing
        like a pair of high boots,
ready to walk me
        back into the fray, what I wanted
was miraculous

        healing—
with a single, pointing
        finger.

Isn't this how I know

      I'm American? The absence of the sniper
on top of the wall?
      The absence of the sniper
for God and Country?
      Isn't it more true here, madness being
exactly that,
      gunned down without pretense in the back
of the post office, the sole living clerk playing dead
      under a desk—

But the hiss of the mind, saying
      There must be a reason. The hiss of the mind:
Was he high?
      Was he black?
What do you see
      when you look in the face of your
Polish neighbor?
      The wife of the commandant
who put your great aunts in ovens?
      You don't know
whose photographs sit on top of her mantle—
      you don't know the hates
hoarded up in her heart—

      I was

nailing a map of the world to the floor, over the exact spot
      where the dishwasher was
in the haunted restaurant below. It seemed
      that I lived up there, over the place
where just a moment before

a fork came flying at my throat—
I had been on the street. I went in
        to alert the owner,
I knew there was a ghost

        inside.
Glass plates
        in the dishwasher shattering, nobody near them, glass
shattering—I was

        nailing a map of the world to the floor,
the protective gesture,
        I was trying to keep it away, the ghost,
lumbering up out of his emotional stupor
        to Shut Us Up,
to command my sister
        to clean out the dishwasher though it was my
balking turn,
        and *the unfairness of it* she wept enraged
until he stood,
        red-faced and hollering, bare feet planted on the kitchen floor,
juice glass shattering in his hand—

        I was nailing a map of the world, of the world—
Where every night is the night
        my sister took a fork to my father's throat.

III

In the air
        a cloth whipping up,
a black flame buffeted through the shrapnel and violets—
        the grenades
stopped.
        And you, grabbing that leg by its booted heel,

struggling to pull it from the sucking muck,
     as if you could retrieve
a man,

     whole—
Look up.
     To the black shroud arcing on the wind, to see
the sky
     let out like a sheet,
flapping clean and bright over the corpse of the country, it's
     Spring,
bloodstains are seeping into the ground
     and coming up poppies
between the burned-out trunks of the trees—
     Where is this place
I'm calling a country, is it here on the highway,
     is it there
in the shot heart
     on the poppied field, what I wanted
was miraculous healing,
     what I wanted—

I was driving, the news kept playing, the limbless, the fractured,
     civilians and factions
spilling out of its cornucopia of grief and divide,
     diffusing and spreading themselves black
between the buildings
     shooting a dose in a flesh-pink sky, the stars
firing off lights from their swelling synapses over the cabs thrumming
     down the Westside Highway as the commandos advanced
on the hospital trenches
     where I stood in a gown in the ditch-brown water, in my head
I had seen myself descend,
     in my head—

to be the given shield.

Country of one.

What had I gone there to save.

THE PROBLEM OF LIGHT

Sunray cutting the dark cloud in two, that lucky lit patch
of land—

The soul,
that cramped dark thing,
       in the body
bitten and chained—

The problem of light.

The problem of it,
flaming down
       against the punched out panes of the abandoned mill, the sudden
pigeon lit like the splaying of a hand, opening
       in the derelict
dark—

where the children are sleeping.

In a litter of beer cans, and cigarette butts, dreamless—

You want to enfold them in great wings, feathered mother.

To lift them.

All day they're asking for change, shoplifting doughnuts
from the grocery store—

You want the beam to come down, love's election.

The beam to come down—happy end.

The problem of light, so perplexing, darkness seems its only
solution—

The darkness
of the abandoned mill, ray of light
    striking down through it—

    creeping up on her arm
flung out from the blanket, palm up and open, light filling it like liquid
    poured—

    as the children sleep—

    as she scrambles up
with her arms huddled round her, then blinks into her open palm—

    and squints up at the window, bright, shattered, glass-tips winking
as the shaft skewers down, keeping her,
    electing her,
making her
    awake.

EXIT,
     blood-red beacon in the dark.
The screen gray like smoke, gray
     as a scrim of ash,
the red curtains furling round it like flames.
     Red curtains, red walls, red seats and carpet, even our faces
under red-reflected shadows—
     Me and two kids and a man.
Sunny outside, unbearable.
     Sunny,

after five days of rain, the day demanding
     to be entered and filled,
the clouds having dropped from its enormous
     shoulders,
and the duty, to be present for it,
     to say My what a fine summer day . . .

     The lopped-off fifth of Cinema Five, pinky
masquerading
     as a hand—

     I went in, I waited, for the flashes and burns
of another blockbuster, for the requisite explosions
     and hip bon mots,
for the red aesthetic
     slaughter—

     And the two kids: what did they want?

A little chaos, a little blood
	to make their day, their unpredictable fragmented day—
And the man,
	what did he want?
O long tunnel out of despair, distraction of someone else's
	story—

But the waiting, the silence,
	the red.
Like a dark, like a lullaby—
	like a cave.
Because wasn't there the urge to something sacred in it,
	the cars and kids and hysterical sirens
unable to penetrate
	the air-conditioned vessel where we sprawled or slumped,
mute,
	inviolate, prima materia
for the chemic operations
	of thunder and light in the pitchman's hands, O
Arnold, Disney, Mafia two-step, make us, make us
	be—

something else for awhile.
	Or nothing else for awhile, a series of stunning self-
destructions: point A
	where we slit our throats, point B where the paper shredder
churns us up, and
	C the slash, the cuffs, the gun, all evil bloodied
and done—

	like a dark, like a lullaby—

	to slake the blood-urge to the drum, the dance,
the hypnoid figures made alive in the fire

(71)

of crowding torches
wavering in the stink of the kill —

the spirit in the spirit pictures come —

when there was something there, to lick it all up,
something to pray to, to fear,
        to appease —

It was sunny, unbearable, after five days of rain, I couldn't stand it,
        the riot
    of good-mornings-so-beautiful, I went
to the movies, my collusion, consolation, twenty minutes early
    before the first bad preview
rated G for its violence and complete lack of sex, rated G
    for us,
the general audience, me and two kids and a desolate-looking man,
    we went in,
we waited, for the flashes and burns of the next great escape
    from the tyrannous day
called Thinking and Feeling, in the lopped-off fifth
    of Cinema 5,
the three black blocks on the dark red walls
    a plastic fleur-de-lis —

To give up the burden awhile.
    To be an eye.
Perceiver.
    God of the kingdom.

BANISHING THE ANGELS

And then the cloud passed and a light came rushing down the steps

of the subway, and blazed up against the phone booth

standing in the corner, and inside it was a girl

talking on the phone, all lit up amid the grime

of the subway, and when I saw her I wanted her to be

an angel, I wanted her with wings inside the station, to say

"the angel on the phone" and see it softly beating, old newspapers

at its feet and no one noticing, white and gold in the dirty glass,

blazing religious in the piss and exhaust, an oddity bright in the life

of the phone booth, an angel in a box in the filtered sun,

where I was straining to look back at the light rushing down,

at the girl who was not an angel talking on the phone,

in the real light of the unmystical sun, thinking

the girl who is not an angel is something to believe—

the phone booth in the sunlight, something to believe—

Different park, different day.

Different park (same), different day (same),
     different different—

She's a girl, no
she's a woman, no

she's a man.
Human Being. Amphora.
Vessel of bone
     and blood . . .

It was the day, the gray damp day in a week of rain and her walk
     to work—

so fine his head in the sky with the darkening clouds, ripping the sky
     like the sky was paper, his head—

in the dripping bracken, morning mist bathing his face.

Watching how her heels are modest,
     how they stick a little
each time she lifts them from the sopping grass, how she does not know
     she is animal—

     as he is, sniffing—

     for that hint of scent, that bright how-are-you through the misted
morning, and she is

so slow crossing the grass, the pace that clicks, yes,
so he emerges,
     the drip from the willow as he brushes past
tinkling like little bells—

to say Excuse me, do you know the time?

Excuse me do you know where a pay-phone is?

     And you,
at the far far fountain, stopping to tie your shoe.

Looking up to see the couple stopped on the field, already the narrative
     at work in your head,
Goodbye my darling, see you at six, until she points in the direction
     of the subway station
and they walk off, together, kindness, encounter, her first real blush
     in fifteen years
humming through your head as they vanish down the slope,
     the new sap burning like blood—

     in the trees, where he is pushing her—

     into the trees, into the *real story*—

     where she's knocked to ground crying *Dios donde*—

     crying to the sky to see it, to say Yes I see it,
          God, hand
     at the controls, I see it—

     but her angels, they won't be returning.
     Hidden on high they won't be returning.
     You and me, we're supposed to be the angels now.

The Work

Ice, burning off the river in the crystal air—
    Souls lifting.
Rapture.
    As you want to see it.
Lifting and then vanishing in crowds, as if a door's being shut,
    as if a door's being shut though there are ever more
crowds of souls
    waiting to rise, above the glass and steel towers erect above the river,
their deserted floors lit and their elevators ready
    for the nothing that will show up all day—
The antenna lights on top of them, red and twinking, city,
    hard as stars.

    You're in it, in the hardness and vapors.

    In the unbreakable, the ungraspable.

    Hurrying against the light, truck horn blaring, bearing down

    and fading, down the desolate Sunday avenue.

    Six o'clock
in the city of hidden dragons, exhaling the remnants of their hidden fires
    through the rotting piers and ice-edged grates,
smoldering beneath the river and under the streets, in the lungs,
    yes,
of you—

The sun edges, reluctant, to the rim of the eastern shore.

You walk and breathe, watch your soul lifting.

II

The cherubs chipped and worn at the lintels,
        the gargoyles at the cornices, the saints on the dashboard
of the taxi
        idling at the light—

Idling,
        at the *light*—

Idling—

        at the curb of the street where the bodies are tucked
into newspapered corners and tarp-covered stoops,
        their boxes and bags and sleeping shadows
dusted with a thin coating of ice—

        14 degrees and the mercury dropping.

        14 degrees and the mercury

lifting up on his icy wings, up and up past the rusted steel railings
        of the fire escapes,
all the six flights to the rotting gap
        between the window and the frame of your box
apartment,
        and slipping, soundlessly, in—

        What will he take, god of thieves?
        What will he fix, caduceus?

Had you felt him perched at the foot of your bed as you tossed,
sleepless and dream-plagued,
        as you stood and groped down your ill-lit stairs,
pushing open the heavy-locked door—

        and hurried into the knifing air,
past the bodies asleep in the vapors obscuring the padlocked stores
        and vacant lots,
to stop transfixed at the steaming river, its slow exhalation of souls—

        so cold, the red tips of your fingers, the little white crystals
at work in your blood, your gloveless hands jammed
        into your pockets
as you watched the sun come cold.

And turned back, reluctant.

And trudged up the steep flights.

And turned the key in the lock.

And stepped in—

III

This is it: America—
        You put the water in the pot.
This is it: your century—
        You put the match to the stove.
You can feel it, the city, constant around you, as you put the dark tea
        in the cup.

What is the river, what are the souls, to the engine of industry
        grinding about you,

to the tightening weave of the electronic strings
     on which love and money and science are speeding,
to the ghost bodies iced on the frozen stairwells, what are they,
     your river and souls?

Radiator's hiss.
Droplets at the pot's rim bubble and vanish.
And what is this, to your river and souls.

I V

Tea now. Drink it.
     Little hearth in your hands.
Water and salt, my vessel, my loved one, are making their marriage
     again.

     To say, I hurt—
     To say, The heavens are empty—
     To say I hurt, the heavens are empty, the streets are empty,
          beer cans scatter, the click and tink of their tinny bells—

     To say there is a Dark Age grasping for light, extending its bent
          hands back to the other one, which had striven and striven,
     while this one doesn't even know
          it strives—

     And to say, The sirens are advancing.
     And to say, It's 1999.
     And to say, My gas bill is late.
     And to say, There is no lover.

     And to rise up to the stove and pour the water in the cup,
to watch the tea stain it,
     while mercury opens his doctoring wings and hovers

(80)

at the edge of the ceiling,
        to cocoon you,
to give you a stage—

        it is the work, Sophia, wisdom, jewel,
        it is the work.

Dana Levin grew up in Lancaster,
California, in the Mojave Desert.
A 1998 Pushcart Prize Winner and a 1999
recipient of an NEA fellowship,
she has also received grants and awards from
the Academy of American Poets, the Vermont
Arts Council, the Vermont Studio Center,
the Ucross Foundation, and New York University,
where she graduated from the
Creative Writing Program in 1992.
She teaches at the College of Santa Fe.

CPSIA information can be obtained
at www.ICGtesting.com
Printed in the USA
JSHW031949140422
24886JS00005B/7